JACK'S STORY

Laverne Spivey

To order additional copies of this book, contact:
Xlibris
844-714-8691
www.Xlibris.com
Orders@Xlibris.com

ISBN: Softcover   978-1-4363-3813-4
        EBook   978-1-6641-3678-6

Library of Congress Control Number: 2008903743

Print information available on the last page

Rev. date: 10/14/2020

I went to the store that morning and bought dog and cat food. I took the food to the shelter at lunch time. I have never seen so many animals. They were in pens and cages everywhere. Around the inside of the building and the outside. Scared, helpless animals all over the place. And it was hot, so very hot Some of the animals were panting very heavily and their tongues were hanging out. As I was leaving I noticed a little dog. He was so scrawny but he seemed to be smiling at me. He looked so bad that I knew he had been through a lot I thought I am taking that little dog home with me.

When I went inside the shelter there were people and animals everywhere. People were signing up to take the animals home with them until the true owners could take care of them. As I was standing there waiting my turn with a new dog in my arms, I remembered that at home I already had two dogs. One is real old with many medical problems which demands a lot of my attention. So with tears in my eyes I decided I would leave that poor dog at the shelter and think about it

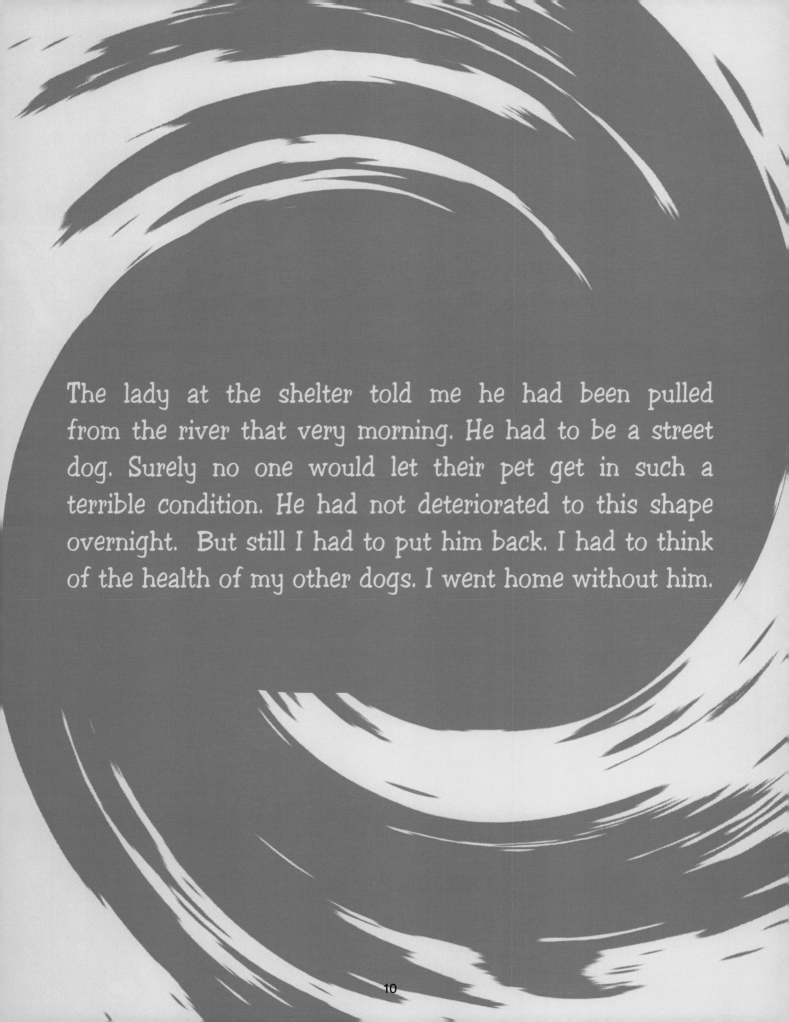

The lady at the shelter told me he had been pulled from the river that very morning. He had to be a street dog. Surely no one would let their pet get in such a terrible condition. He had not deteriorated to this shape overnight. But still I had to put him back. I had to think of the health of my other dogs. I went home without him.

All afternoon I thought of that little dog. He was so lonely and scared. All he needed was tender loving care and a good home. I looked at my dogs and thought about how lucky we were to have each other Two hours later I made up my mind. I went back to the shelter to get the little dog. I can't explain why I went back for him. It wasn't because he looked good. He looked terrible, but he couldn't help how he looked. What life he lived was terrible. He had no home, and no one to feed and take care of him.

When I drove up to the shelter he was sitting in the cage waiting. I began talking to him I told him "I am taking you home with me." He was smiling and was so happy. I am going to name you Jack. Jack Flood. After some paper work and a rabies shot we started home. Jack sat in the front seat looking at me then looking ahead. Smiling all the time and thinking, she is a nice lady. I knew she would come back for me.

Jack was so run down anemic. He was covered with fleas. I tried to give him a bath but he was terrified of the water. Who could blame him? He was skin and bones and fleas.

JACK The nice lady put food down for me. I ate and ate until I waddled away. Too tired and too full to eat anymore. The next day we went to the vet. I weighed eight pounds. I had lots of worms and fleas and very little hair. Almost all of my hair had fallen out because of the fleas. After three months and many treatments I had gained weight and strength, now I look like a real dog. In fact I am a cocker spaniel mix and proud of it

I love my nice lady and my new home. I am so happy now and I have lots of hair. My lady friend wouldn't get my hair cut for a long time because for so long I didn't have much hair. I was two years old when the nice lady changed my life. I weigh 25 pounds now. I am a big boy. When my lady friend asks "do you want to go to McDonalds"? I am ready.

We were born under an old house where no one lived. Our mother was a good mother. She loved us very much. I have a brother and a sister and we loved our mother We were big enough we could run and play and we stayed close to each other. One day our mother went out to find food and she didn't come back We had no mother to take care of us any longer. I was so depressed. I missed her so much. I was afraid something bad would happen to us. We were so hungry. We survived eating what we could find in the alleys and streets. We tried to stay together but somehow I got separated from my brother and sister.

I was all by myself from then on. I had no one and I was afraid and lonely. Days and nights went by and I was so very hungry. Before I knew it I was surrounded by water. I couldn't see land anywhere. I was so weak. Knowing I couldn't survive long. It took all my strength to keep swimming and keep my head above water. Then I heard something. A boat with people in it They were talking. They saw me and were coming toward me. They finally got to me and were pulling me out of the water and into the boat. I was so thankful. There is good people who care. They carried me to the shelter.

I am so thankful I went back to the shelter for this little dog. My poodle Coco died a few months after I brought Jack home. He knows he is special. Jack and Morgan my border collie, sleep with me and have a real close relationship themselves. Jack is 16 years old now. His health is real good and we have a good life together. I miss him every hour I am away from him. Jack is a little spoiled but he loves it. Jack likes children and other animals. He is just perfect. Since he is getting older he likes to take a nap in the afternoon. Jack likes to go for rides and to McDonalds for a burger. Often while we are riding he will reach over and give me sugar as if to say "thank you". There is a special bond between "Jack the Flood Dog" and me.

Printed in the United States
By Bookmasters